MY FAMILY STORY
Told and Examined

A Workbook to Accompany
FAMILY THERAPY
An Overview
Fourth Edition

Irene Goldenberg
U.C.L.A. Neuropsychiatric Institute

Herbert Goldenberg
California State University, Los Angeles

Brooks/Cole Publishing Company

I(T)P™   An International Thomson Publishing Company

Pacific Grove • Albany • Bonn • Boston • Cincinnati • Detroit • London • Madrid • Melbourne
Mexico City • New York • Paris • San Francisco • Singapore • Tokyo • Toronto • Washington

A CLAIREMONT BOOK

Sponsoring Editor: Claire Verduin
Editorial Associate: Patricia Vienneau
Production Coordinator: Dorothy Bell
Cover Design: Roy R. Neuhaus
Cover Photo: The Henry Moore Foundation
Printing and Binding: Patterson Printing

For more information, contact:

BROOKS/COLE PUBLISHING COMPANY
511 Forest Lodge Rd.
Pacific Grove, CA 93950
USA

International Thomson Editores
Campos Eliseos 385, Piso 7
Col. Polanco
11560 México D. F. México

International Thomson Publishing Europe
Berkshire House 168-173
High Holborn
London WC1V 7AA
England

International Thomson Publishing GmbH
Königswinterer Strasse 418
53227 Bonn
Germany

Thomas Nelson Australia
102 Dodds Street
South Melbourne, 3205
Victoria, Australia

International Thomson Publishing Asia
221 Henderson Road
#05-10 Henderson Building
Singapore 0315

Nelson Canada
1120 Birchmount Road
Scarborough, Ontario
Canada M1K 5G4

International Thomson Publishing Japan
Hirakawacho Kyowa Building, 3F
2-2-1 Hirakawacho
Chiyoda-ku, Tokyo 102
Japan

Printed in the United States of America

10 9 8 7 6 5 4 3

ISBN 0-534-33917-4

Cover photo: Sculpture entitled *Family Group*, LH 269, 1948–9. © The Henry Moore Foundation.

PREFACE

All families tell stories about themselves. We Millers love to argue, we Salingers adore children, we Changs have great memories, we Avilas are mathematically inclined. Typically such stories are passed along over generations and are adopted without challenge by new generations.

Sometimes they appear as problems. The Peterson men are mean and self-centered. The Washington women always get involved with the wrong men. The Hardys have always been hard drinkers. The Smiths cannot take pain.

This workbook is intended to provoke you into examining the stories your family has agreed to tell about itself, and especially how these stories affected the adult you became. Through a series of exercises, we hope you will scrutinize the myths and legends, truths and half-truths, realistic self-appraisals and self-deceptions in your family, all in the service of aiding you in understanding many of the beliefs with which you grew up and which influenced your development.

To gain the most from this workbook, you must be honest about yourself and your family. You must also be knowledgeable about basic family concepts as well as the major issues raised by the various theorists and practitioners in the field. If, as you proceed through these exercises, you find that you require further assistance or clarification, refer to *Family Therapy: An Overview,* Fourth Edition, by Irene Goldenberg and Herbert Goldenberg (Brooks/Cole Publishing Company, Pacific Grove, California, 1996). (The exercises in this workbook are organized according to the chapters in the text.) You can also refer to the original sources, listed in the References section of the text, for more detailed reading.

Ideally, the workbook experience should act as a catalyst in your personal growth process. It may serve as a vehicle for finding your strengths and weaknesses as a potential family therapist. Don't hesitate to share self-observations and insights, when appropriate, with professors, supervisors, therapists, parents, or significant others. Should you develop "stuck places" or become troubled by patterns you find about yourself, seek help from someone who thinks in systems terms, understands behavior emerging out of a family context, and who therefore speaks your language.

By learning more about yourself, especially by adopting a family perspective, we believe you can help others, future clients, see themselves within the contexts of their families.

Irene Goldenberg
Herbert Goldenberg

CONTENTS

Chapter 1
Adopting a Family Relationship Framework

The Structure and Patterns of My Family System

1.1. How many generations can you trace back in your family? Did your family keep records, or was the information handed down through a retelling of family history over the generations? How important is your family history to the way you see yourself today?

1.2. Entrance into a family occurs only by birth, adoption, or through marriage. Compare the characteristics of family membership (loyalty, support from others, closeness, etc.) of two people in your family, each of whom joined the family by different routes. How are they different and how are they alike?

1.3. "Family membership remains intact for life." Do you agree or disagree with that statement? Have any of your family members attempted to disengage from your family? What have been the consequences for that individual and his or her role within the family system?

1.4. Family members are irreplaceable owing to the network of emotional ties created between members. Give an example from your life and evaluate its contribution to the role your family plays in your life today.

1.5. In what type of family structure did you grow up—nuclear, blended, one led by a single parent? Did it change over time? Has divorce played a role in your life?

1.6. What is your present family structure? Are you living at home? In a dorm? An apartment off campus? Cohabiting? Examine your own roles. In what ways are they similar to your parent's of the same sex? In what ways different? Did you tell yourself, growing up, that you would seek different patterns (e.g. male-female relationships) than you saw between your parents or between your grandparents? If so, how are they different? Are there any resemblances you hadn't anticipated?

1.7. What are the expectations you have about the family structure you will be part of in five years? Twenty years? Forty years? Include a discussion of your attitudes toward marriage, children, divorce, extended families.

Family Assumptions and Strategies

1.8. Family strategies may be aimed at maintaining a family system, accentuating stress in order to reach a desired goal, or repairing the family's ability to cope with changing internal or external conditions. Discuss at least one such strategy employed by your family. What was its goal? How successfully was the strategy used?

1.9. Most families have an outlook that perceives the world in general as a positive and predictable place or as a dangerous and menacing one. This perspective affects all family members. What was the general world view of your family when you were growing up? How were you affected?

Family Roles

1.10. Draw a picture of your family. Be sure to include all members. When you have finished, note what you see about your view of relationships, alliances, and coalitions within the family.

1.11. List in order of importance the roles that you currently play (son or daughter, friend, student, lover, neighbor, etc.).

1. _____   4. _____

2. _____   5. _____

3. _____   6. _____

Which of these roles are integral to your sense of self (ones you believe you cannot do without)?

Of all the roles listed above, which *one* would you insist on holding on to most strongly?

Of all the roles you have listed as currently playing, which would you find it easiest to give up?

Dyads and Triads

1.12. Dyads represent temporary or sometimes permanent liaisons between people. Within a family, numerous alliances of this kind occur, some lasting a brief period (e.g., during the temporary absence of a key member) and some more or less permanent. List the important dyads in your family. Pay particular attention to ones in which you have participated and to their significance in your adult life.

1.13. Were there any significant triadic or three-person relationships within your family when you were growing up? Following the format of the preceding question, briefly discuss their impact on your life.

1.14. How does making the paradigmatic shift from an individual to a family perspective change the way you view relationships in your family of origin? Does the notion of circularity affect any long-held linear ideas of who did what to whom?

1.15. Provide an explanation of some behavior of yours that has been criticized by a significant family member—first in the language of linear causality and then in that of circular causality.

1.16. Think of a current personal problem you have. How do you understand the origins of that problem in cybernetic terms? What part did your relationship with your family play in the development, maintenance, and perpetuation of the problem?

The Identified Patient

1.17. At different stages of a family's life cycle, different members may be labeled the "identified patient" or symptomatic person. Did this occur in your family? Who was so designated? Did you ever receive that designation? How did it affect your everyday behavior and your picture of yourself?

1.18. Is there currently an identified patient in your family, perhaps labeled "sick" or "bad"? Does this person drain off tension for the family, or distract from other underlying problems? What have you noticed?

How did this designation get established? How could it be changed?

What would happen to the interaction of the remaining family members if this person left?

1.19. No families are problem free; no individual grows up unaffected. In what ways would you consider yourself to have grown up in a "troubled" family? What were the negative consequences for you or each of your siblings? Were there any positive consequences for any family member? What were they? For whom?

1.20. Consider a problem that exists or has existed in your family (say, an adult's drinking problem, or chronic unemployment of a parent, or a child who is a slow learner or one who refuses to go to school). Describe the problem as it is understood in your family.

Now rethink the problem as a possible product of a flawed relationship between two or three family members. Describe.

Did this change how you viewed the problem? How?

1.21. If you told your family story, how would it be different from versions told by your sister or brother? Your mother? Your father?

Frequently, there is consensus among family members about their family story, especially an agreed-upon explanation of how they arrived at where they find themselves today. What is your impression of the factors that went into your family adopting that particular story? What kinds of conversations need to occur in order to change your family's narrative about themselves?

Summary of Chapter Entries   (What did I learn about myself? What needs further exploration?)

Chapter 2

Family Development: Continuity and Change

Your Family of Origin

2.1. Chart your family's life cycle from a developmental point of view. Pay particular attention to any "stuck" places in the cycle where unexpected events (e.g., financial reverses, prolonged illness, an unexpected death) led to particular family problems. What were these problems? Did "symptoms" develop in any family member (e.g., depression, drinking, anxiety attacks)?

2.2. What kinds of relationships are maintained across generations in your family? Do grandparents maintain a special relationship in your family with their grandchildren? What is the significance of those relationships? Do they relate to separation issues?

2.3. Discuss in systems terms the statement that grandparents and grandchildren are friends because they have a common enemy.

2.4. In a marriage, each spouse usually acquires a set of roles and adheres to a set of rules for marital interaction. In your parents' marriage, do you believe these paradigms were resolved so that each individual maintained a sense of self? Elaborate.

Your Current Family Patterns

2.5. What do you hope will be the same or different in your future family compared to your family of origin?

Same as Family of Origin	Different from Family of Origin
_____	_____
_____	_____
_____	_____
_____	_____
_____	_____
_____	_____

Elaborate.

2.6. How does your expected role (as a husband or wife or remaining unmarried) differ from that of your same-sex parent? In what way were your socializing experiences related to this issue different or the same when you were growing up?

2.7. Comparing yourself with your same-sex parent at your current age, what noteworthy differences in expectation exist (e.g., regarding family responsibilities, career moves, child rearing)?

2.8. What were the crtitical transition points for your family of origin (e.g., marriage, birth of first child, last child leaves home)? Were there one or more points of particular crisis involving the resolution of any of these family tasks?

2.9. In many families, adolescents are the focus of much attention, as if they and not the family system are the cause of family conflict. What was going on with your family members at the time of your adolescence that contributed to family harmony or disharmony?

2.10. Interview your mother about her transition from childhood to adolescence. Can she remember any specific problems she had? If applicable, how did your mother's life change when she lost one or both of her parents, or needed to care for elderly parents?

2.11. Interview your father about the same circumstances described in the preceding exercise.

2.12. A common crisis over separation occurs in a family when a child first enters school. Ask your parents whether this crisis occurred in your family of origin, and how the family coped with the situation.

2.13. Describe the stage of life your parents were in when you reached adolescence. How did this affect your adolescence?

2.14. Will you or have you left your family's home to live alone or with others? If so, how have your mother and father reacted to this stage in family development? Are their responses different? How?

2.15. Have you experienced the death of a grandparent? Was it the first death where you were involved? How did your family handle it? What reactions of yours do you recall?

2.16. Overall, how has your family dealt with life cycle transitions? Did they deal with job changes, children leaving home, marriages, illness or death of family members with the same equanimity? Can you remember a transition that was problematic for your family? Was there someone who developed symptoms around that time? Describe. Was the family "stuck" for a period of time? How, and how well, did they move beyond the impasse? Are there any residual consequences today?

2.17. Consider the issue of stress in your family. Did the stress first appear in your parents or grandparents? Were family patterns (e.g., drinking), attitudes (all the men in this family are weak), or secrets (grandma and grandpa never actually got married) passed on to you? What has been their influence on your outlook and expectations?

Intact and Alternate Family Life

2.18. Was your family of origin ever a single-parent-led family (owing to death, divorce, or withdrawal of a parent)? If so, what were the significant consequences for the family (economic hardship, grief, loss of a support system, etc.)?

Gender Issues

2.19. Does your family fit stereotypic gender-determined patterns in its role assignments? Describe.

How do your expectations of dividing up domestic and outside work responsibilities with a mate compare to those of your parents?

2.20. Which of your parents played a more obviously nurturing role in raising their children? Did this activity have high or low status in the family? To what extent is your own degree of nurturing behavior affected by your gender?

Ethnic Considerations

2.21. How were your parents' child-rearing methods affected by their ethnicity and social class status?

2.22. What was the impact of your family's socioeconomic and ethnic background on the development of your current attitudes regarding money, political affiliation, sense of acceptance in mainstream American society, etc.?

2.23. How has your sense of your own ethnicity, racial background, or socioeconomic level growing up affected your future plans?

2.24. Did you grow up with people culturally and ethnically like yourself? If so, how did that contribute to your stability and sense of belonging? If you grew up in an environment where you felt different, how did that affect your sense of yourself and your acceptance by others?

2.25. Which social class best describes the one in which you grew up?

Working class   Middle class   Upper middle class   Wealthy

(Circle one)

How does this background affect your attitudes regarding class differences? Are there areas in your thinking that might affect your ability to work therapeutically with members of classes very different from your own? Any blind spots? Explain.

Summary of Chapter Entries (Pay special attention to the similarities and differences you see in your current or anticipated family life as compared to life patterns in your family of origin.)

Chapter 3
The Family as a Psychosocial System

Family Rules, Family Roles

3.1. All families have certain unspoken rules, such as: no discussion about sex; deny mother's drinking; never raise your voice; if you can't say something nice about someone, don't say anything at all. What were some of the rules in your family of origin?

3.2. What were some of the unspoken but agreed-upon trade-offs between the adults in your family of origin? (For example, that father will be logical and realistic if mother is feeling and sensitive.)

3.3. How was money handled in your family when you were growing up? Who had the right to decide what about how it was spent? In what way is your handling of money different and in what way the same as what you experienced in your family of origin?

3.4. Do you know a family in which the parents, themselves immature, have reversed roles with one of their children, who has taken over the parenting role? Describe the relationships. Can you speculate on the future of the child who takes on parenting functions prematurely?

3.5. Scapegoats within a family go under many guises. Do you recognize any of these in your family?

idiot _____   mascot _____   wise guy _____
fool _____   clown _____   saint _____
malingerer_____   black sheep _____   villain _____
imposter _____   sad sack _____   erratic genius _____

Describe the behaviors of the persons labeled. What were the consequences for that individual's role in the family later in life?

3.6. Crises occur in all families. Some are resolved relatively quickly, others linger. Describe two such situations in your family—one in which homeostasis was restored quickly, another in which resolution was more difficult.

3.7. Has separation of one family member from the others in your family provoked a crisis? This can occur due to illness, death, vacation, business, war, etc. What happened? How was homeostasis restored?

3.8. What do you see as the next developmental crisis for yourself (e.g., getting married, having a baby, divorce)? Discuss how your family structure will be affected. What family homeostatic mechanisms do you anticipate will be called into play?

3.9. What homeostatic or corrective operations are you aware of engaging in currently when dealing with a quarrel with a loved one, in order to reduce intense anger and return to a quieter state?

Morphostasis and Morphogenesis

3.10. A tightrope walker must continually sway to remain balanced; to remain balanced while standing in a canoe calls for making the canoe rock. Add a couple of people on the tightrope and a few in the canoe, and you will begin to understand how difficult it is for a family to remain balanced but also to change in a rhythm that will help individual members adapt. Add some environmental pressures (wind; going over rapids), and the problems can become monumental.

What hazards has your family been able to negotiate and still remain balanced?

Family Feedback Mechanisms

3.11. How do you signal for attention with someone you care about? Verbally? Nonverbally? Is this tactic different or the same one you used as a child?

3.12. What kind of positive and negative feedback do you get from friends or current family members? Be specific.

3.13. Trace the feedback loops that occurred after a misunderstanding between two members of your family. Was the subsequent exchange of information used to correct or escalate the problem?

Subsystems and Boundaries

3.14. Were you aware of important subsystems that existed in your family when you were growing up? Describe them. Were they organized primarily by generation, gender, alliance against another family member or faction, or by a similar dimension?

3.15. How permeable was the parental boundary when you were growing up? What effect did the relative openness or closeness of your family system have on your development?

3.16. What macrosystems were significant in the life of your family (church, social agencies, health care programs, etc.)? Discuss.

3.17. When larger systems (e.g., the school) defined the problem of a family member differently than the family did, how did your family attempt to resolve the contradictions? How successful were they in doing so?

Summary of Chapter Entries (Include what you have learned about the rules and roles as well as the homeostatic and feedback mechanisms in your family. How well does your family cope with crisis? How does your family system mesh with larger social systems?)

Chapter 4
Origins of Family Therapy: A Historical Perspective

Individual vs. Family Therapy

4.1. Safeguarding the personal privacy of the therapist-patient relationship has been a cornerstone of psychoanalytic treatment. Family therapy, in contrast, is sometimes observed directly by others or videotaped for later viewing by trainees and supervisors or by professional groups. This brings up the issue of confidentiality. What are your feelings about participating with your family under the conditions of family therapy?

4.2. What are your feelings about sharing your "secrets" with your family members and a therapist? Any reservations? Any family taboo topics? How would you expect your parents to respond to these questions?

A Systems Outlook

4.3. A seven-year-old child is doing poorly at school. How are each of the following systems affected?

Organ System (The Nervous System) _____

_____

Organismic System (The Individual) _____

_____

Group System (The Family) _____

_____

Organizational System (The School) _____

_____

Societal System (The Neighborhood) _____

_____

4.4. Referring to the preceding question, offer your suggestions for positive intervention to change the situation.

4.5. Describe your own "world" in living systems terms. Be sure to comment on as many levels of subsystems in the hierarchy as you can in order to show relationships between levels (cell, organ, organismic, group, etc.).

4.6. Think of a problem in a family member, such as periodic despondency or bursts of aggressive behavior, and "explain" is at:

    a. the individual level

    b. the family level

    c. the societal level

4.7. Were any of the following patterns recognizable in your family of origin? Circle any that are applicable.

Marital skew   Marital schism   Emotional divorce

Discuss their consequences for the other members of your family.

4.8. "Emotional divorce" was an adaptive technique that was probably more common before actual divorce became easier. What examples, if any, are you aware of in your family history? Would that same adaptation occur today? If not, why not?

4.9. Although double-bind messages occur in disturbed families, they also occur in normal ones. Can you give an example of a transaction from home, school, or work where you were double bound? What did you do? What was the accompanying affect? What would happen had you tried to interrupt the sequence?

4.10. Analyze some problematic behavior of yours (e.g., nail biting, smoking, overeating, swearing) from an intra-psychic viewpoint and then a family therapy perspective. What has changed? Where is the locus of pathology?

4.11. Trace a conflict or problem you currently have back to a grandparent.

4.12. Trace a strength or skill you have in a similar way.

4.13. Describe a family you know, saw on television, or read about in a book in which the members appear loving and understanding, but on closer observation are actually separate, distant, and unconnected. What happens to a child in such a pseudomutual family?

Marital/Family Therapy

4.14. Marital counseling was a precursor to family therapy. Did your family have or could they have profited from marital counseling? Which of the following personal problems might they have discussed?

Spouse: marriage
Child: relationship with child
Other family relationship problems
Job, school, or vocational problems
Situational problems—death, illness, financial reverses

4.15. List the kinds of group therapy you have experienced yourself or known someone closely who has been involved:

Psychodrama _____

_____

Group therapy _____

_____

Human relations group (T. Groups) _____

_____

Encounter groups _____

_____

Tavistock groups _____

_____

Others _____

_____

4.16. What positive and/or negative changes came from this experience?

4.17. What are your personal attitudes toward group or individual therapy? Which would be better for you? Why?

Summary of Chapter Entries   (Be sure to include a discussion of yourself and your family from a problematic viewpoint.)

Chapter 5
The Growth of Family Therapy: 1950–Present

The Founding of Family Therapy

5.1. Suppose you have sought help for a symptomatic family member in the 1950s, and the therapist proposed the revolutionary idea that your entire family attend the sessions. Describe the reactions of as many of your family members to this proposal as you can.

5.2. How would your family feel if they were approached to participate in a research project on family functioning? Are there specific members who would be enthusiastic and others who would be defensive and resistant?

5.3. How would you feel about being observed through a one-way mirror as you interacted with your family members? Would some pose or try to be on their best behavior? Would others tend to dominate or control the session? What would your behavior likely be at first?

5.4. List as many advantages to brief therapy as you can.

5.5. What are the pros and cons of teaching parents "behavioral management skills"?

5.6. Knowing yourself, if you were a therapist, which would you be, a conductor or a reactor? Why?

5.7. Assume there is a symptomatic member of your family, who all agree is the identified patient. You all agree further to attend a session if it would help him or her. However, it soon becomes clear that the therapist is focusing on family interactions, not the patient's individual problems. How would you react? What would it take to persuade you to participate in further sessions?

5.8. How effective would family therapy be with your family of origin? Why?

5.9. List in two columns the values that had the highest and lowest valences in your family of origin. Include the following (and any others you wish to add) in your list.

Autonomy
Nurturance
Control
Independence
Relationships
Dependency
Caretaking

HIGH VALUE   LOW VALUE

_____   _____

_____   _____

_____   _____

_____   _____

_____   _____

_____   _____

Did your family approve of attributes commonly associated with males or females equally, or was one emphasized over the other? Explain.

5.10. How was power distributed in your family? Who was in charge of what? What role did gender play in that assignment?

5.11. Name and describe some ways in which a gender-based rule or sexist attitude or stereotypic sex role assignment affected the kind of adult you are.

5.12. Where do you stand on the aesthetics vs. pragmatics issue in family therapy? To which sort of therapist would you prefer to go? Who would be most helpful, both in the short run and the long?

Summary of Chapter Entries (Include a discussion of yourself and your family from a gender- and power-related viewpoint.)

Chapter 6
Psychodynamic Approaches to Theory and Practice

The Psychoanalytic Viewpoint

6.1. Should family therapists emphasize the past or present, in your opinion? Explain your position.

6.2. What part did role complementarity play in your family as you were growing up? Describe, and compare to your current relationships.

6.3. Did scapegoating occur to one or more of your family members while you were growing up? What were the lasting results of such a role designation? Are there any current residuals in that person's relationships to the rest of the family?

6.4. A woman resumes a career as her children enter high school. What potential failures in role complementarity may be expected? Discuss each member in a hypothetical family (or a real one if you know such a family), emphasizing how each must modify existing roles.

6.5. Did any sudden role changes occur for any family member as you were growing up? What circumstances (e.g., death or disability of a major wage earner; widowed grandmother moves in) led to the change? Describe how the various members of your family reacted.

6.6. Choose your own or a friend's family and describe any "interlocking pathology" between the parents that you have observed. How have you or your friend dealt with possible entanglements or side-taking? How successfully?

6.7. Try to imagine what it would be like to go to a therapist with a psychoanalytic viewpoint together with your parents or others in your family of origin.

a. What are your initial reactions?

b. What are your expectations of what would transpire?

c. Who would benefit most? Why?

6.8. If you presently are in a relationship that has developed problems, would it be better or worse if your spouse or significant other attended the psychodynamically oriented therapy sessions with you? Explain.

Object Relations

6.9. Consider the statement that an individual's capacity to successfully function as a spouse depends largely on that person's childhood relationships to his or her parents. Applied to yourself, what expectations might you have about your own marriage or other long-term relationships?

6.10. What "introjects" left over from early childhood relationships are you aware of in yourself today? What impact do such imprints have on:

a. current dealings with adults

b. current dealings with children

6.11. Observe two mothers with their infants. What diffences do you notice about their attachments? What part does each play in maintaining the attachment? If the infant is securely attached, what effect might that have on his or her future adult relationships?

6.12. Have you ever witnessed what the object relations theorists call "projective identification" taking place between partners? If so, describe and comment on its ultimate impact on their relationship.

6.13. Object relations theory emphasizes the fundamental human need for attachment. Being in a relationship is underscored, as are the possible destructive effects of early separation from caring figures.

a. Discuss this from your own experience.

b. Consider the working mother who places her child in a day care arrangement. What would object relations theorists consider the potential problems?

6.14. Robin Skynner calls unrealistic anticipations of others based on unfulfilled developmental needs (e.g., a lack of mothering) "projective systems." People use spouses or children to recreate situations to satisfy these needs. Consider the mother who tries to make her child mother her—or the husband who tries to get his wife to mother him. Are there situations like this that you can identify in your family? Describe.

The Contextual Viewpoint

6.15. Boszormenyi-Nagy understands the "context" of a family to include the past, present, and future of the family, especially its dynamic and ethical interconnections. What resources can you find from the past history of your family that sustain or enrich your life today?

6.16. In your family's ledger, what are some of the "unpaid debts" or restitutions that need to be made? If mother worked to put father through school, has she been repaid? Was there an imbalance in child-care responsibilities? Was that debt erased? If not, what are the residuals?

6.17. Family legacies dictate debts and entitlements. What legacies did you inherit? Were you expected to be an athlete, a musician, a scholar, a failure, beautiful, etc.?

6.18. How have you carried those legacies or entitlements into your current relationships?

6.19. How have any past family legacies you have brought into a current relationship been in conflict with those brought by your spouse or significant other? How have you sought to "settle accounts"?

6.20. Can you trace any of those legacies back to a grandparent? Discuss.

Summary of Chapter Entries (Take advantage of the chance to express your own theoretical viewpoints as well as to explore the impact of your past family history on your present family functioning.)

Chapter 7
Experiential/Humanistic Approaches to Theory and Practice

The Symbolic-Experiential Viewpoint

7.1. Carl Whitaker works with the emotional infrastructure of the family, using symbols and metaphors to help a family change. Has the use of these devices in art, literature, or poetry provided you with insight or otherwise affected your behavior? Be specific.

7.2. What does "psychotherapy as a growth experience" mean to you? Would that definition more likely invite your participation or make it less appealing?

7.3. Do you favor a therapeutic endeavor that attempts to uncover the past or one that addresses the immediate moment-to-moment encounter with an active and involved therapist? Explain your position.

7.4. What advantages and disadvantages do you see for yourself and your family in a co-therapy situation?

7.5. Whitaker has been described in the text as iconoclastic—and sometimes outrageous—in dealing with families. He is unpredictable, and uses humor, his own fantasies, and unconscious processes, even falling asleep, to contact and challenge his clients. How would you and your family respond to such an approach?

7.6. Have you ever experienced a time in your life when "acting crazy" was a liberating experience?

7.7. How would you feel about having your grandparents (separately or together) in a family therapy session with you and your parents? What special problems would arise? What problems would most likely be avoided? Who would be most helped?

7.8. Whitaker has a number of "rules" for "staying alive" as a human being and as a therapist, as described in the text. One is to "enjoy your mate more than your kids, and be childish with your mate." Was that true for your parents? Describe.

7.9. If you personally have experienced any psychotherapy, think about whether growth and change occurred primarily in the therapist's office or outside. Discuss.

7.10. A Gestalt therapist characteristically avoids taking a formal family history. What effect would that have on his or her understanding of your family? In your family's case, would it be better if certain historical material were known early on by the therapist, or not?

7.11. How would your family react to a therapist's confrontational efforts to help them try to become more spontaneous and expressive of their feelings, both within the family and with outsiders?

7.12. Learning to communicate "I" messages is a basic exercise for Gestalt family therapy clients. For example, instead of an accusatory "You never pay attention to me!" an "I" message might be "I'm feeling ignored by you and it's upsetting me." Talk to a significant person in your life and be sure to make "I" statements. How does the transaction change?

7.13. Has someone in your family had a symptom (overweight, school refusal, alcoholism) which the family attacked directly? What happened?

7.14. Which would be more comfortable for you and your family, a therapist who was self-revealing or one who was not? Why?

The Human Validation Process Approach

7.15. Sometimes a phenomenological perspective (looking at family behavior from within the system) can make what appears to others to be "crazy" or "stupid" or "self-destructive" appear understandable and appropriate. Can you give an example from your experience?

7.16. Do you have a preference about whether a therapist you and your family choose:

a. belongs to a specific discipline (psychiatrist, psychologist, social worker, religious counselor, etc.)? Why?

b. is a particular gender? Why?

c. is a member of a specific ethnic group? Why?

7.17. Virginia Satir classified family communication patterns in the following way, according to the textbook:

Placater Super-reasonable Congruent

Blamer Irrelevant

Describe the members of your family of origin or your current family using these categories, paying particular attention to each person's *characteristic way* of interacting.

7.18. Satir believed body posture reflects a great deal about an individual. In what way do you cover up your true feelings when you become distressed or feel insecure? What physical pose do you assume?

7.19. Form a group of three persons in your classroom: two strangers and yourself. Each person should choose a new first name. Then decide on a last name and assume a family role. Stay with your same sex role, but do not necessarily stay in your real life family (a son can be a father, etc.). Your communication should be as follows:

Pick a communication style and maintain it.

If you are a blamer, begin each sentence with statements such as "You are never," "You are always." Find fault.

If you are a placater, take the blame for everything that goes wrong. Make sure no one gets hurt. Never say what you want.

The irrelevant one must not communicate in words properly. Be distracting.

The super-reasonable one must be stiff and proper. Stick to the facts, ignore feelings or greet them with statistics.

Have a discussion for five minutes. Stop. Relax. Report any messages you might be receiving from your body. What has happened in your new family? How did it make you feel? Share your impressions with one another and with the class.

7.20. Satir typically presented herself as a model of clear communication. She claimed to tap the nourishing potential in each family through one or more of the following levels of access: physical, intellectual, emotional, interactional, contextual, nutritional, spiritual. To which would your family respond most positively? Which least? Explain.

Summary of Chapter Entries   (Include a discussion of your views regarding the experiential/humanistic outlook, as well as how you and your family might profit, therapeutically, from such a "growth experience.")

Chapter 8
Bowen's Approach to Theory and Practice

Family Systems Theory

8.1. Where do you fit, in relationship to your family, on Bowen's theoretical Differentiation of Self scale? Remember that people at the low end are emotionally fused to the family and thus are dominated by the feelings of those around them. At the other extreme of the scale, the high end, people are able to separate feelings from thinking and thus retain autonomy under stress.

Place yourself on the scale below and explain your answer.

1	25	50	75	100
Fusion				Differentiation of Self

8.2. What scores on Bowen's scale would you assign:

   a. your mother?

   b. your father?

   c. your oldest sibling?

   d. your youngest sibling?

Elaborate.

8.3. Triangulation is often noted in the relationships among children. Can you remember a circumstance from your childhood when a third person was drawn into a relationship to decrease the intensity and stress between the dyad? What happened to the third person?

8.4. In your present family, does triangulation take place? If so, provide an example. Who is the person most likely to be triangled in when conflict arises between two other family members? Why?

8.5. Some of the ways Bowen suggests a family has of dealing with tension are as follows: (1) physical or emotional dysfunction in a spouse; (2) overt, chronic, but unresolved marital conflict; and (3) psychological impairment in a child.

Were any of these present in your family? Discuss.

8.6. Which of the children in your family, when you were growing up, was most fused to your parents? Can you speculate on why that particular child?

8.7. We all wish to differentiate appropriately from our families of origin, but sometimes we cut ourselves off emotionally or geographically from our families without resolving our emotional difficulties. Bowen calls this emotional cut-off. Has this occurred in your family? Describe.

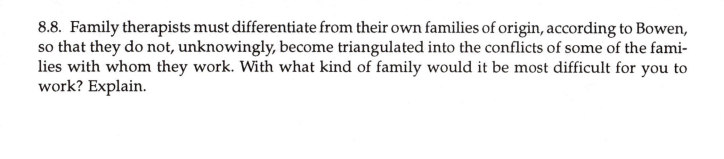

8.8. Family therapists must differentiate from their own families of origin, according to Bowen, so that they do not, unknowingly, become triangulated into the conflicts of some of the families with whom they work. With what kind of family would it be most difficult for you to work? Explain.

8.9. Following the premise in the preceding question, with what kind of family could you most easily and objectively work? Why?

8.10. Bowen's concept of the multigenerational transmission process includes the idea of the selection of a spouse with a similar differentiation level as one's own. Describe a family of origin and their offspring whom you know where you have been able to observe this process.

8.11. What is your sibling position in your family of origin? How does it match the sibling position of the significant person in your life (spouse, roommate, lover, boyfriend or girlfriend)? For example, are you both oldest children who assume responsible leadership roles? Both youngest? One oldest, the other youngest? How do your corresponding sibling positions affect your relationship?

8.12. Observe two pairs of friends with different sibling positions. How are their relationships influenced by growing up in different birth orders in their families?

8.13. Think about the birth order of your mother and father in their respective families of origin. How influential do you think this factor has been in determining the nature of their relationship?

8.14. There is a great deal of difference between a selfish person and a well-differentiated person. Think of two people who fall into these two categories. How are they different from one another? Elaborate.

8.15. Observe an argument between two people you know. If you are drawn into the argument, attempt to stay in contact with both people, but remain emotionally disengaged. Observe how this changes the circumstances. Is it difficult to do? How do you feel about yourself?

8.16. Would your family of origin have preferred a therapist who was controlled and cerebral or one who was emotionally provocative and confrontational? Explain why.

8.17. Make a genogram of your family, covering at least three generations.

8.18. What have you learned about relationships within your family from the genogram? Does seeing it on paper help clarify any family issues?

Family Intervention Techniques

8.19. Circle the term that best fits you when you try to change a friend's behavior.

1. Coach   4. Counselor

2. Therapist   5. Change Agent

3. Family Counselor   6. Advisor

Explain.

8.20. Framo brings family of origin members into his sessions, while Bowen is more prone to send clients home for frequent visits, having coached them in their differentiation efforts. Which would be best for your family? Why?

Summary of Chapter Entries   (Take a transgenerational viewpoint in summarizing what you have learned about your family's influence on your current behavior patterns.)

Chapter 9

The Structural Approach
to Theory and Practice

The Structural Viewpoint

9.1. Minuchin contends that a change in family organization must occur before a symptom in a family member can be relieved. Has such a situation occurred in your family? Who manifested what symptom, and what family restructuring helped alleviate the problem?

9.2. Each family system is made up of a number of interdependent subsystems. List some of the subgroupings in your family

    a. by age:

    b. by sex:

    c. by outlook or common interest:

9.3. Which of the above bases for an alliance or coalition is most influential in determining how your family functions (i.e., carries out day-to-day activities, communicates, negotiates differences, plans for the future)?

9.4. Has anyone in your family ever exhibited psychosomatic symptoms? How did the family deal with the problem? What homeostatic devices were activated whenever that person become ill or developed symptoms?

9.5. List the family subsystems in which you participate. How does your role differ in each?

9.6. Is there any conflict between subsystems in your family that is particularly damaging or destructive to overall family functioning (e.g., older people dismiss what younger people have to say; females believe men are insensitive)?

9.7. Under stress, does your family become more enmeshed or more disengaged? Describe and explain the behavior consequences.

9.8. The boundaries of a subsystem represent the rules defining who participates and what roles each will play in the transactions necessary to carry out a particular family function. In a well-functioning family, the parental subsystem is strong but flexible. How was the parental subsystem in your family?

9.9. Structuralists believe all well-functioning families should be organized in a hierarchical manner, with the parents exercising more power than the children, the older children given more responsibilities than their younger siblings. Was this the case in your family of origin? What were the consequences of the power arrangements when you were growing up?

9.10. Power in a family is rarely absolute, but comes about through an alignment of forces. What person (or groups) had the most power in your family? Why?

9.11. Strong generational boundaries do not permit grandparents to take over parental functions. How did that mechanism operate in your family?

9.12. Did detouring coalitions (in which parents hold a child responsible for their conflicts with each other) ever operate in your family as a way of reducing parental stress? Explain.

9.13. In growing up, most people think about what kind of parent they will be, and how they would do some things differently and some things the same as their parents. How would you be different in your parenting style from your same-sex parent (e.g., handling money, giving affection, imposing discipline)?

9.14. Following up on the preceding question, how would your parenting style be the same as that of your same-sex parent?

9.15. Structuralists use family mapping to depict a family's structure at a cross-section of time. Using Minuchin's symbols described in the text, draw a map of your family at a particular critical time in its existence, paying special attention to the clarity of boundaries, to coalitions, and to ways of dealing with conflict.

9.16. Discuss how you have "joined" or "accommodated" to a friend's or spouse's family that was different from your own.

9.17. If you were to "restructure" the family system in which you grew up, what would be the most important change you would seek: change in rules, change in alignments, change in the distribution of power, etc.? Explain.

9.18. Reframing the meaning of certain behavior can provide a fresh perspective and make that behavior more understandable or acceptable. Reframe the following:

a. Mother pokes into my private affairs too much.

b. Father frightens the family when he drinks too much.

c. Sister is selfish and only thinks of herself.

d. Brother gets away with murder because he's the youngest child.

9.19. List some behaviors in a friend that are bothering you. Then try to reframe the meaning of the behavior so a new outlook results.

BEHAVIOR	REFRAMING
1. That girl is irritating me with her questions.	She would like to make contact with me.
2. _____	_____
3. _____	_____
4. _____	_____
5. _____	_____
6. _____	_____

9.20. How does the reframing in the preceding question change your feelings about the bothersome behavior? Explain.

Summary of Chapter Entries (Pay particular attention to family organization, coalitions, subsystems, and boundaries and the influence of family structure on family functioning.)

CHAPTER 10
Communication/Strategic Approaches to Theory and Practice

The Interactional Viewpoint

10.1. Communication takes place at both the verbal and nonverbal levels. Describe a recent incident in which you were involved where the message you received at one of these levels contradicted the message you were receiving, simultaneously, at the other level.

10.2. List as many nonverbal expressions of interpersonal communication as you can (e.g., shrugging, finger pointing, grimacing), indicating the underlying message to the other person or persons.

10.3. Every communication between people has a content/report and a relationship/command aspect. For example, Dad's comment, upon sitting down to dinner, that the salt is missing from the table may also represent a command for Mom to go fetch it. Can you recall an experience between two of your family members where seemingly innocuous content messages also reflected commands?

10.4. Was the communication pattern between your parents primarily symmetrical or complementary? How did it enhance or constrict their relationship? Illustrate.

10.5. Describe the sort of relationship definitions (symmetrical or complementary) you tend to get into with:

a. your male friends

b. your female friends

c. your parents

d. younger people

e. older people

10.6. What is your characteristic way of behaving with a member of the opposite sex to whom you feel attracted (e.g., aggressive, shy, flirtatious, aloof)? What role do you typically seek as most comfortable and familiar?

10.7. "Disregard this notice" is a double-bind message. "Sex is dirty, save it for someone you love" is another. What double-bind messages are you currently receiving? Are you aware of any you are sending?

10.8. At what point in your life could you and your family have benefited from brief (six-session) crisis intervention? (For example, you might consider divorce, death, drugs, alcohol abuse, school separation, or an auto accident as possible crisis times.) Describe the situation and explain why you believe such intervention might have been helpful.

10.9. Can you think of problems your family attempted to resolve through first-order changes (within the existing system) when second-order changes (restructuring the system) were called for? Elaborate.

10.10. Think of two situations in your life when your family was experiencing a series of problems—one where a time-limited approach utilizing a therapeutic paradox might have helped, the other where long-term efforts aimed at improving the family's problem-solving skills would have been more effective. Describe the situations.

10.11. "Going along with the resistance"—neither confronting the problem nor offering interpretations in an effort to force the family to face the issue—is a technique frequently used in brief therapy. In your own life, describe a situation where someone used this approach with you. Did it work? Why or why not?

10.12. Haley believes that symptoms frequently are indirect strategies for controlling a relationship while at the same time denying that one is voluntarily doing so (e.g., mother becomes ill when adolescent wants to go out for the evening). Can you cite any examples from your own experiences?

10.13. Observe two people in your family deciding an issue, such as priorities for spending money or which movie to attend that night, and describe what you learn about how each defines their relationship.

10.14. Implicit in every relationship is a maneuver for power, according to Haley. What power struggles are still going on in your life?

10.15. Can you picture yourself, as a strategic family therapist, "prescribing the symptom" for a family coming to you for help for a member with insomnia or a handwashing compulsion? How easy or difficult would it be? What special problems would arise for you?

10.16. Paradoxical tasks are used by Haley and others when families are especially resistant to change. Can you imagine an area in your family's life where change might have been beneficial but was resisted by the family as a whole? How might paradoxical interventions by a therapist have helped?

10.17. Suppose a friend of yours smoked too much, drank too much, or swore too much, and came to you for help in ridding himself of such excesses. Can you think up a therapeutic double-bind, a symptom prescription, or a paradoxical intervention to aid in reducing or eliminating the symptom?

10.18. What would your reaction be to a therapist who used prescribing ("practice being depressed") or restraining ("go slow") as paradoxical techniques in working with you or your family?

10.19. According to strategists, anxiety attacks, phobias, and heavy drinking are sometimes indirect and unacknowledged ways used to control what occurs between people. Can you think of a similar symptom in one of your family members that controlled the behavior of one or more of the other members of the family?

10.20. Can you design a prescriptive paradox addressing the symptomatic behavior of someone in your family? Describe how you go about it and what results you would expect.

Summary of Chapter Entries (Include a discussion of what you have learned about your family's communication patterns, relationship definitions, and possible responses to strategic interventions.)

Chapter 11

The Milan Systemic Approaches
to Theory and Practice

The Systemic Viewpoint

11.1. Bateson defined information as "a difference that makes a difference." What new information introduced into your family (perhaps through talking openly about a family secret) might have changed family members' behavior toward one another? Speculate on the changes.

11.2. Do you know of families whose unacknowledged "rules of the game" allow them, together, to control one another's behavior? Describe their efforts to perpetuate such "games." How effective is this maneuver in sustaining their relationships?

11.3. A family agrees to attend family sessions, but insists that the therapist treat only the symptomatic member because the rest of the family is fine. If you were the family therapist, how would you proceed?

11.4. You finally persuade your family to come for family therapy as a group, hoping the therapist will expose the family "games," which only you seem to acknowledge. Instead, the therapist offers positive connotations about behavior patterns you believe are destructive, as he or she warns the family about premature change. How would you react?

11.5. Would "long brief therapy" be effective with your family of origin? What would be its advantages and disadvantages?

11.6. What would be the effect on you or your family of seeing a therapist and being observed from behind a one-way mirror by a team of his or her associates? How would you react to the intersession in which the therapist leaves the family alone while consulting with those colleagues?

11.7. Describe a dominant and long-lasting rule in your family of origin and speculate on what it would take to change it. Who would be most upset by the change?

11.8. Consider any symptomatic behavior that occurred in any member of your family while you were growing up (school problem, chronic illness, parent-adolescent conflict). Describe the family's "explanation" of the problem, and then offer a positive connotation that reframes the problem. What would have been the reaction of various family members had such a reframing been suggested?

11.9. How were birthdays celebrated in your family of origin? Was the person celebrating the birthday treated in a special and predictable way to mark the occasion? Were symbols (cards, gifts, ceremonies, family dinners) a part of the ritual?

1.10. What were the rituals surrounding the evening meal in your home when you were young? What topics could be discussed? What topics were avoided? Did people sit in specific places on a regular basis? Was food ever used as reward or punishment? Who was served first?

11.11. Rituals often play a central role in family life, marking passages and changes. Prescribing rituals may help a family restructure how its members perceive events. In your family, describe a ritual (wedding, birthday party, graduation, funeral) that helped your family negotiate a change.

11.12. Following up on the preceding question, describe a ritual that was unsuccessful in bringing about the desired change, and speculate on the reasons for its failure.

11.13. List some questions about a problem in your family which draw attention to differences in perception among family members (e.g., who was the first person to notice the problem?). How would such questioning change the family's thinking?

11.14. Discuss the difference between a therapist being inactive, indifferent, or neutral. In a family argument, where you do not want to take sides, what are some techniques for remaining neutral?

11.15. Picture yourself as a systemic family therapist. How comfortable would you feel offering a directive in the form of an invariant prescription? With which kinds of family problems would it be easier, which more difficult?

11.16. If the technique of invariant prescription had been applied by a therapist to your family when you were young, what do you think would have resulted? Consider possible negative as well as positive changes.

Summary of Chapter Entries (Here is a chance to pay special attention to any important family "games" that influenced family development when you were growing up.)

Chapter 12
Behavioral/Cognitive Approaches
to Theory and Practice

Applying Behavioral Concepts

12.1. Select a family problem you have discussed earlier in this journal and restate it in behavioral terms.

12.2. Take the family problem you have now redefined in behavioral terms in the previous exercise and:

a. Discuss its frequency and length.

b. What antecedent and consequent events are associated with the problematic behavior?

c. What environmental contingencies support and reinforce the behavior?

d. Discuss the specific responses to the behavior by various family members.

12.3. Think of someone with whom you currently have a strained relationship. Speculate on the origins of the problem using behavioral concepts.

12.4. Following up on the preceding question, what suggestions can you make for reshaping the interaction so that it becomes more positive and satisfying to both of you?

12.5. Try to shape someone's behavior by giving him or her positive reinforcements (a smile, a kiss, a gift, attention) whenever desired behavior occurs, while ignoring undesired behavior. Continue to do this for seven days. Describe your results and draw conclusions.

12.6. Cognitive psychologists pay specific attention to how individuals organize, store, and process information. Consider a problem you may have had for a long time, and put it into words at these three levels: automatic thoughts, underlying assumptions, and schemas or basic core beliefs. How would you go about treating the problem from a cognitive viewpoint?

12.7. Behaviorists sometimes use the phrase "quid pro quo" (something for something) to describe how couples in a successful marriage work out a suitable arrangement for exchanging pleasures. Take a look at your parents (or an uncle and aunt) and try to describe the range and frequency of the reciprocal positive reinforcements they exchange.

12.8. Could your parents have benefited from help in learning "marital skills"? Which of these five skills—more effective listening, greater self-expression, proper forms of request-making, exchange of feedback information, and seeking clarification of the other person's message—do you believe would have been most beneficial? What role would "acceptance of partner" have played?

12.9. Although the exchange of positive reinforcements between intimates sounds ideal, many people have trouble taking the "positive risk" of giving such a reinforcement before receiving one. What difficulties would exist for you in such a situation?

12.10. Create a "caring days" list with a significant other in your life. Be specific in your requests and ask the other person to be the same in his or hers. Exchange the lists. After one week, note any changes in the relationship.

12.11. Were there any surprises in the "caring days" requests you received in the preceding exercise? How did such surprises alter your perception of the relationship and/or change your subsequent behavior?

Behavioral Parent Training

12.12. Was there significant problematic behavior (eating, sleeping, being disciplined) in one of the children in your family as you were growing up? If so, describe the situation and speculate on how it might have been handled more successfully (or with less stress) if your parents had received behavioral parent training?

12.13. Would a contingency contract have been helpful in resolving any conflict you may have had with your parents when you were an early adolescent? Describe the problem briefly and set up a contract.

12.14. Did your parents use informal methods of reinforcing desired behavior (e.g., promising a bicycle if your grades improved significantly)? How well did such methods work? Did they create any problems?

12.15. Observe a current family problem between members of different generations. Perform a functional analysis of the problem. Be sure to include what elicits the problematic behavior, what helps maintain it, and precisely how the interaction between the family members involved reflects their coping styles and efforts.

12.16. Establish a contract between yourself and a family member or friend. Begin by determining a common problem between the two of you, then negotiate a solution. Provide for reinforcers and negative consequences that are acceptable to both of you. Describe your problem, procedures, and results.

12.17. Functional family therapists regard an individual's behavior as always serving the function of creating specific outcomes in that person's interpersonal relationships. Observe a friend or family member over several days, noting behavior patterns (without regard to whether you consider them desirable or undesirable), then speculate on the function of the behavior.

BEHAVIOR   FUNCTION

_____   _____

_____   _____

_____   _____

_____   _____

_____   _____

Elaborate.

12.18. Consider a seemingly dysfunctional pattern between two members of your family, but one that nevertheless has become chronic. What interpersonal payoffs might exist for the participants that help perpetuate the pattern?

Conjoint Sex Therapy

12.19. What was the dominant sexual theme transmitted to you by your parents (e.g., sex is a natural and enjoyable part of life; sex is to be endured; sex is not to be discussed). What has been its impact on your current attitudes toward sex? What will you transmit to your children?

12.20. Would a couple you know who is contemplating seeking help for a sex problem feel more comfortable with a behavioral or a systems approach? Explain.

12.21. Under what conditions would you decide to send a couple for marital therapy or for sex therapy?

Summary of Chapter Entries   (Emphasize behavioral/cognitive concepts in describing the origin, maintenance, and possible extinction of problems within your family.)

Chapter 13

Early Models and Techniques of Family Therapy

Family Group Therapy

13.1. How would your family of origin have reacted to a therapist such a John Bell? Compare their willingness to attend further sessions after initial sessions with Bell and with at least two other therapists described in the text.

13.2. In your class, pick a group of people to represent your family members. Place them physically to show their relationship to one another. Discuss with the class the tableau you have created.

Change their positions to show how you would like them to be.

What did you learn?

13.3. Observe on videotape two people in a conversation about a neutral subject. Watch for nonverbal messages expressed through body language. How congruent is what is communicated at the verbal and nonverbal levels?

13.4. Observe the same two persons discussing an emotionally charged subject. What changes in communication pattern, verbally as well as nonverbally, do you detect? Discuss.

13.5. Turn off the sound on a television dramatic program or daytime soap opera in which family interaction is taking place. Can you identify any choreography patterns that communicate something about the nature of current family interactions? Describe.

13.6. If your family has made home movies, observe interactions at different stages of the life cycle and comment on any changes you may observe in the transactional patterns.

Crisis-Oriented Treatment Procedures

13.7. You enter a clinic with a problem person in your family. Your family is in great distress. You are told that you will have to commit yourselves for 2 to 2½ days of intensive scrutiny. What would be the positive aspects of this experience for you?

13.8. Regarding the simulated Multiple Impact Therapy experience in the preceding exercise, what would be the negative aspects you envision?

13.9. Imagine that you had a family member who was experiencing an acute schizophrenic episode. You take him or her to the local psychiatric hospital, where you are told that two options exist: hospitalization for an as yet indeterminate period or outpatient treatment. In the latter case, you are informed that the entire family will be involved in the treatment, which will involve six sessions over the next three weeks. Which would you choose? Why?

13.10. Your grandfather becomes seriously depressed. He lives with you, and family life has become destabilized. The therapist to whom you bring him insists after several individual sessions that a family crisis is occurring and that you must all come to his office on a weekly basis to resolve the crisis. How would your family react? What are some of the pros and cons of this approach from your viewpoint?

Large-Group Treatment Procedures

13.11. Multiple marital couples therapy, like all forms of psychotherapy, is usually conducted by trained leaders or facilitators. Suppose three couples you know decide to meet weekly on their own to talk over common problems, without a therapist. Discuss the possible advantages and disadvantages of such a plan.

13.12. Learning new patterns for resolving one's family conflicts may come from observing another family deal with an analagous problem. Some non-therapy group examples are Al-Anon, a family support group for a family member who is alcoholic; nursery school observation groups, where parents observe and then discuss the children's behavior; and Marriage Encounter, where couples have an opportunity to observe other married people solve their problems. Visit one of these programs and report back to the class on what you identify as the major change agents.

13.13. Design a social network intervention for someone you know who has a drug or alcohol problem. Whom would you include in the network? What would be the advantage of such an approach? What special problems do you foresee?

13.14. If you have participated in a social network group (e.g., a religious group, dorm, fraternity or sorority, boy or girl scout group, cousins club, fraternal organization), describe what happens when the group turns its attention to the problems of one member.

Summary of Chapter Entries (Be sure to include your reactions to as many of the forms of family intervention as you can.)

Chapter 14
New Directions in Family Therapy

14.1. Postmodern therapists no longer invest their faith in truth and objectivity. Imagine your family going to such a therapist. Would they want an expert, or someone with whom to talk out their problems together? Which members would you say preferred which type of therapist? Explain.

14.2. The feminist critique has helped identify certain patriarchal biases inherent in many of the basic assumptions and practices of family therapy. How would these biases affect therapy for your family? Would some members prefer a feminist approach? Which ones? Why?

14.3. Psychoeducationists emphasize interpersonal skill-building, a technique especially suited for seriously dysfunctional families. Can you think of a family you know where such an approach would be the treatment of choice? State your reasons.

Postmodern Constructivism

14.4. Postmodern thinking has helped focus interest on diversity and pluralism in society. What issues of ethnicity, race, social class, and sexual orientation were important to your family when you were growing up? How did these affect your current attitudes and behavior regarding these issues?

14.5. Postmodernists consider constructions regarding reality to be based on language and communication. How is your mother's or father's picture of you based on your description of yourself? How different are their views from one another, and from that of a friend who has known you a short while?

14.6. Different opening remarks by a therapist are likely to establish different sets and thus elicit different responses from the family. How would you respond to each of the following?

a. Tell me what problems brought you to see me today.

b. How can we work together to help change your situation?

14.7. How have you reacted to someone who has attempted to help you overcome a problem of yours (overeating, smoking, not studying) by urging you to pay attention to your positive behavior (those times when you don't overeat, etc.) rather than focus on the undesired behavior?

14.8. Answer this version of the "miracle question" for yourself:

"Suppose that one night there is a miracle and while you were sleeping the problem that you have been worrying about is solved. How would you know? What would be different? What would you notice the next morning that would tell you a miracle had occurred? What would your best friend notice?"

14.9. Create and describe a hypothetical collaborative solution-oriented dialogue between members of your family and a therapist. Be specific regarding who would say what to whom.

14.10. Describe a problem that has existed in your family and consider the proposition that it was created through language and could be deconstructed or dissolved through language.

14.11. Think of a problem you have had in your family where the attempted solutions always seemed to bring more trouble. Can you identify a "unique outcome"—a time when you took some action and the problem did not get worse? What was different about that set of circumstances? What can you learn from the experience?

14.12. Have a small group discuss a problem while the class watches. Then have the small group watch while the class discusses reactions to what they observed. Reverse the procedure once more. What did you learn?

14.13. Examine your attitudes regarding the roles of men and women in a family. How do these attitudes reflect what you learned in your family of origin, and how are they different?

14.14. Describe the degree of flexibility or rigidity of sex roles assigned in your family when you were growing up.

14.15. What are your views regarding the recent interest in men's groups whose members meet to nurture and expand their awareness of what it means to be "masculine"? What do you believe might be the positive or negative outcomes?

Medical Family Therapy

14.16. Has there been a medical problem that affected the life of a member of your family? What kind of help of a psychological nature might have helped the family? The afflicted member? What kind of help did you actually receive?

Summary of Chapter Entries   (Be sure to address postmodern techniques, gender-sensitive issues for your family, and psychoeducation where applicable.)

Chapter 15

Research on Family Functioning and Therapeutic Interventions

Family Research Methodology

15.1. By now you have some ideas about why families interact in the way they do. What further research questions would you like to see addressed? State your questions or research proposals in systems terms.

15.2. Describe an area of family functioning you are interested in investigating and design a qualitative research methodology to carry out your plan.

15.3. Take a position on the applicability of traditional research methods to the study of family systems. Defend your viewpoint.

15.4. You are doing a research study on dysfunctional families and need a normal baseline for comparative purposes. How would you go about defining a "healthy family"?

15.5. How would you rate your family of origin in terms of communication deviance when you were growing up? Would you say the rating changed over time?

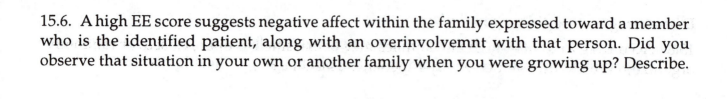

15.6. A high EE score suggests negative affect within the family expressed toward a member who is the identified patient, along with an overinvolvemnt with that person. Did you observe that situation in your own or another family when you were growing up? Describe.

15.7. Would you describe your role in your family of origin as more that of a therapist (actively intervening in family functioning) or a researcher (observing, classifying, and evaluating what was transpiring)? How did that earlier role influence your current interests?

15.8. According to Kantor and Lehr, families may be classified as open, closed, or randomly organized. Which did you personally experience as a child?

15.9. Following up on the preceding exercise, did you have a friend in a different type of family organization? How did his or her experiences appear to be different from yours?

15.10. Which of Reiss's family paradigms comes closest to the pattern of your family of origin? Illustrate how your family members dealt with a crisis, based on the type to which you have assigned them.

Family Measurement Techniques

15.11. Where would your family of origin fit in Olson's Circumplex Model? Select one of his 16 types of family systems most like your own and explain your choice.

15.12. If your family were to come for family therapy, would you want the therapist to diagnose them? If yes, should he or she share that diagnosis with the family? If no, why not?

15.13. Look at the structure of the place where you work or attend school. Would you characterize the climate as rigid or flexible, autocratic or democratic, competitive or cooperative? How does this climate affect your functioning?

15.14. Observe a family planning something they will do together as a group (go to a movie, go on vacation, etc.). How much information can you gather about the power structure, communication patterns, and degree of family functioning? Discuss.

15.15. In regard to your family of origin, rate the degree to which the system was characterized by the open expression of feelings.

1.0	1.5	2.0	2.5	3.0	3.5	4.0	4.5	5.0
Open, direct expression of feelings		Direct expression of feelings despite some discomfort		Obvious restriction in the expression of some feelings		Although some feelings are expressed, there is masking of most feelings	No expression of feelings	

15.16. Discuss whether yours was a centripetal or centrifugal family in terms of separation styles. Did each of your siblings use the same style in leaving the family? Explain.

Family Therapy Process and Outcome Research

15.17. Address the general question "Does psychotherapy work?" In what circumstances, for whom and under what conditions do you think it would have worked for your family?

15.18. Where do you stand in the debate over the relative merits of process versus outcome research? Defend your position.

15.19. What aspect of family therapy research would you like to continue to explore? Research methodology? Theory building? Classification and assessment? Process or outcome research? Explain your position.

Summary of Chapter Entries   (Your views and judgments of family assessment and therapy research, especially as applicable to your family, are important here.)

Chapter 16
Becoming a Family Therapist: Training and Supervision

16.1. How have your personal experiences, family history, and schooling influenced whether you have an individually focused or family-focused view of the causes and treatment of maladaptive, problematic, or dysfunctional behavior?

16.2. Try to determine your personal objectives in becoming a family therapist. List them in descending order of importance.

1. _____

2. _____

3. _____

4. _____

5. _____

Elaborate.

Obtaining Clinical Training

16.3. Training in marital/family therapy today occurs in three kinds of settings: degree-granting programs in family therapy, freestanding family therapy training institutes, and university-affiliated programs. What do you see as the special benefits and shortcomings of each? Which fits you best?

16.4. Should a family therapist in training be required to undergo a therapeutic experience with his or her family? Take a position on this issue and defend your point of view.

16.5. Family therapy can be viewed as a profession, an orientation to human problems, or simply as another therapeutic modality. Which outlook most closely reflects your position? Explain.

16.6. For you, which would be a better learning experience: (a) a single integrated approach to family theory and practice, or (b) learning a variety of family therapy theories and techniques? Explain your position.

16.7. Having surveyed the various approaches to family therapy described in the accompanying text, which holds greatest appeal for you? Why? Consider both intellectual content and style of treatment in your answer.

16.8. According to Cleghorn and Levin, three sets of learning objectives must be fulfilled in order to develop basic therapeutic skills with families. Rate yourself on the following three skills dimensions:

Perceptual Skills

1	2	3	4	5	6	7

Do not do well.
One of my weak behaviors.

Acceptable behavior
in this area.

Very good. One
of my strong
points.

Conceptual Skills

1	2	3	4	5	6	7

Do not do well.
One of my weak behaviors.

Acceptable behavior
in this area.

Very good. One
of my strong
points.

Executive Skills

1	2	3	4	5	6	7

Do not do well.
One of my weak behaviors.

Acceptable behavior
in this area.

Very good. One
of my strong
points.

16.9. What personal qualities of yours are your greatest assets in becoming a family therapist? Do you have any special qualities that may hinder your effectiveness with families?

Supervision

16.10. What do you see as the major advantages and disadvantages of a supervisor going over a videotape of you working with a family?

16.11. Consider yourself as entering therapy along with your family members. What feelings would you or the others have about being told that the session would be recorded for later viewing by a supervisor?

16.12. If you were receiving live supervision as you worked with a family, which of the following would be most comfortable for you? Which least comfortable? Why?

1. Telephone call from supervisor who offers suggestions

2. Bug-in-ear as you conduct a session

3. Supervisor enters therapy room

4. Calling you out during a session for consultation with a team that has been observing you and your client family

16.13. Would you prefer to work alone with a family or with a co-therapist? Explain. If you had a co-therapist, what personal qualities would be important for that person to possess? Would the sex of your co-therapist matter? Why?

16.14. Some client families are more anxiety-provoking for some therapists than others. What kinds of families would be most difficult for you to work with (e.g., aggressive, silent, secretive, demanding)?

16.15. What kinds of families would you feel most comfortable with? Consider social class, family communication style, religion, or other relevant factors.

Summary of Chapter Entries   (Be sure to include a discussion of what you believe would most help you personally in becoming a family therapist.)

Chapter 17
Professional Issues and Ethical Practices

Licensing

17.1. In seeking professional help, what questions would you ask a potential provider regarding licensing? In your opinion, to what extent does licensing of family therapists serve a useful public function? Can you muster any strong arguments against licensing?

17.2. How would you go about selecting a family therapist for yourself and your family? Would you seek out any specific discipline? What fee would you expect to pay? Should that fee be more than for individual sessions? How should lengthier sessions, if needed, be billed?

17.3. How would you feel if your family therapist had to consult with another therapist to determine the number of sessions the family could come for therapy?

17.4. Your family's health insurance is handled through a managed care arrangement. You select a family therapist from their provider list, but are told that confidentiality cannot be guaranteed absolutely, since after several sessions the therapist must report details of the treatment to a case manager in order to receive authorization to continue. How would you respond? What are your options?

17.5. Do you know of a therapist who has been accused of sexual misconduct with a patient? What were the circumstances? What effect did this information have on your sense of trust in professionals?

17.6. Working as a family therapist, you see a family for an initial session and become concerned that one family member appears suicidal. How would you proceed?

17.7. What are your views regarding therapist record keeping? Would you feel comfortable as a client if the therapist took extensive notes during the session? Brief notes? No notes at all?

Maintaining Ethical Standards

17.8. Suppose you learn from a family that they were seen previously by a therapist who, according to their statements, abandoned them when they could no longer afford treatment. What are your professional responsibilities in this matter? What are your options? How would you proceed?

17.9. You learn from a friend that the family therapist you are seeing has been sanctioned several times for advertising infractions and has received a final educative warning. How would you deal with the matter?

17.10. You tell a therapist you are seeing together with your family that you cannot afford his fee. He says not to worry, that he will bill your insurance company as though each family member came to see him separately, and the total billing will more than pay for the sessions. Would you agree to this plan? If not, what would you do?

17.11. Would you like to talk to a family therapist alone before your family sees her? What advantages or disadvantages does this present?

17.12. What strong religious, political, or philosophical attitudes or values do you hold that might affect your functioning as a family therapist?

17.13. A major ethical issue in family therapy concerns whose interests should be the primary concern of the therapist. The identified patient? Only the members attending the sessions? The family? Society? Explain your viewpoint.

17.14. Take a position regarding the handling of secrets in family therapy. In your opinion, should family members ever be seen individually if they want the therapist to be informed but feel they cannot divulge certain secrets to other family members at that time?

17.15. A client asks if what he is about to tell you will be kept in confidence. If not, he adds, he will not divulge the information. Can you guarantee confidentiality? If not, what would you say?

17.16. Would the fact that a therapist cannot testify in court about what you reveal to him in confidence have any bearing on your willingness to speak freely? Explain.

Summary of Chapter Entries (Be sure to include your views regarding specific aspects of professional practice as well as ethical issues.)

TO THE OWNER OF THIS BOOK:

We hope that you have found *My Family Story: Told and Examined, A Workbook to Accompany Family Therapy: An Overview, 4th Edition*, useful. So that this book can be improved in a future edition, would you take the time to complete this sheet and return it? Thank you.

School and address: _____

Department: _____

Instructor's name: _____

1. What I like most about this book is: _____

_____

_____

2. What I like least about this book is: _____

_____

_____

3. My general reaction to this book is: _____

_____

4. The name of the course in which I used this book is: _____

_____

5. Were all of the chapters of the book assigned for you to read? _____

   If not, which ones weren't? _____

6. In the space below, or on a separate sheet of paper, please write specific suggestions for improving this book and anything else you'd care to share about your experience in using the book.

_____

_____

_____

_____

_____

Optional:

Your name: _____ Date: _____

May Brooks/Cole quote you, either in promotion for *My Family Story: Told and Examined*,
or in future publishing ventures?

Yes: _____ No: _____

Sincerely,

Irene Goldenberg
Herbert Goldenberg

BUSINESS REPLY MAIL

FIRST CLASS   PERMIT NO. 358   PACIFIC GROVE, CA

POSTAGE WILL BE PAID BY ADDRESSEE

ATT: *Irene and Herbert Goldenberg* _____

**Brooks/Cole Publishing Company
511 Forest Lodge Road
Pacific Grove, California 93950-9968**

NO POSTAGE
NECESSARY
IF MAILED
IN THE
UNITED STATES